A TRUE BOOK™

My United States

Utah

JOSH GREGORY

Children's Press®
An Imprint of Scholastic Inc.

Content Consultant

James Wolfinger, PhD, Associate Dean and Professor
College of Education, DePaul University, Chicago, Illinois

Library of Congress Cataloging-in-Publication Data
Names: Gregory, Josh, author.
Title: Utah / by Josh Gregory.
Description: New York : Children's Press, [2018] | Series: A true book | Includes bibliographical references
and index.
Identifiers: LCCN 2017053984 | ISBN 9780531235829 (library binding) | ISBN 9780531250952 (pbk.)
Subjects: LCSH: Utah—Juvenile literature.
Classification: LCC F826.3 .G74 2018 | DDC 979.2—dc23
LC record available at https://lccn.loc.gov/2017053984

Photographs ©: Ezra Shaw/Getty Images; back cover: Howie Garber/age fotostock; back cover ribbon: AliceLiddelle/Getty Images;
3 bottom: Stefan Auth/imageBROKER/age fotostock; 3 map: Jim McMahon/Mapman ®; 4 left: FLPA/Ignacio Yufera/age fotostock;
4 right: Ovydyborets/Dreamstime; 5 top: Pavliha/iStockphoto; 5 bottom: Tom Hanson/AP Images; 7 center bottom: zrfphoto/
iStockphoto; 7 center top: Richard Cummins/Getty Images; 7 top: ferrantraite/iStockphoto; 7 bottom: Pierre Leclrc/Shutterstock;
8-9: johnnya123/iStockphoto; 11: Kenneth Keifer/Shutterstock; 12: Brian K. Miller/age fotostock; 13: Larry Gevert/Dreamstime;
14: kwiktor/iStockphoto; 15: Darren Bennett/age fotostock; 16-17: AndreyKrav/iStockphoto; 19: Eli Lucero/The Herald Journal/
AP Images; 20: Teguh Mujiono/Shutterstock; 22 left: Atlaspix/Shutterstock; 22 right: Sakda tiew/Shutterstock; 23 center: FLPA/
Ignacio Yufera/age fotostock; 23 bottom right: Spectruminfo/Shutterstock; 23 top center: Geografika/Dreamstime; 23 top right:
Ovydyborets/Dreamstime; 23 top left: Markuk97/Dreamstime; 23 bottom left: Simm49/Dreamstime; 24-25: Babak Tafreshi/Getty
Images; 26: Kojihirano/Dreamstime; 29: Everett Collection/age fotostock; 30 bottom right: thisbevos/iStockphoto; 30 top left:
Kojihirano/Dreamstime; 30 top right: Everett Collection/age fotostock; 30 bottom left: Babak Tafreshi/Getty Images; 31 bottom:
Library of Congress/Corbis/VCG/Getty Images; 31 top right: Tom Hanson/AP Images; 31 top left: Atlaspix/Shutterstock; 32: Andreas
Feininger/Library of Congress; 33: Mathew Brady/Sarin Images/The Granger Collection; 34-35: Per Breiehagen/Getty Images;
36: Rick Bowmer/AP Images; 37: Dia Dipasupil/Getty Images; 38: Rick Bowmer/AP Images; 39: Scott G Winterton/The Deseret
News/AP Images; 40 inset: Paul Brighton/Dreamstime; 40 background: PepitoPhotos/Getty Images; 41: A Held/age fotostock; 42
top left: Robert Picard/INA/Getty Images; 42 top right: Ron Galella/WireImage/Getty Images; 42 bottom left: Jacques Bourguet/
Sygma/Getty Images; 42 center: Adolph/ullstein bild/Getty Images; 42 bottom right: Bobby Bank/WireImage/Getty Images; 43 top
left: Paul Sakuma/AP Images; 43 top center: Al Messerschmidt/AP Images; 43 top right: Jeopardy Productions/Getty Images; 43
center: Joe Martinez/PictureLux/age fotostock; 43 bottom left: Ivan Nikolov/WENN.com/age fotostock; 43 bottom right: Michael
Boardman/WENN.com/age fotostock; 44 center left: Johnny Adolphson/Shutterstock; 44 top: Pavliha/iStockphoto; 44 center right:
GEORGE FREY/AFP/Getty Images; 44 bottom: benedek/iStockphoto; 45 top right: legacyimagesphotography/iStockphoto; 45 center: Idpeacev/Dreamstime; 45 top left: Mel Kowasic/Shutterstock; 45 bottom: Mathew Brady/Sarin Images/The Granger Collection.

Maps by Map Hero, Inc.

1 2 3 4 5 6 7 8 9 10 R 28 27 26 25 24 23 22 21 20 19

**Front cover: Red Bull Rampage
mountain bike competition
Back cover: Bull moose**

Welcome to Utah

UNITED STATES

←Utah

Find the Truth!

Everything you are about to read is true **except** for one of the sentences on this page.

Which one is **TRUE**?

T or F Brigham Young was the first European explorer to reach Utah.

T or F Utah was once a part of Mexico.

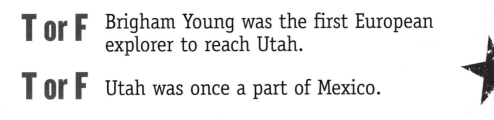

UTAH

Y46 1EN

LIFE ELEVATED

Find the answers in this book.

Contents

1 Land and Wildlife

2 Government

THE **BIG** TRUTH!

Cherries

What Represents Utah?

Rocky Mountain elk

Arches National Park

Snowboarder

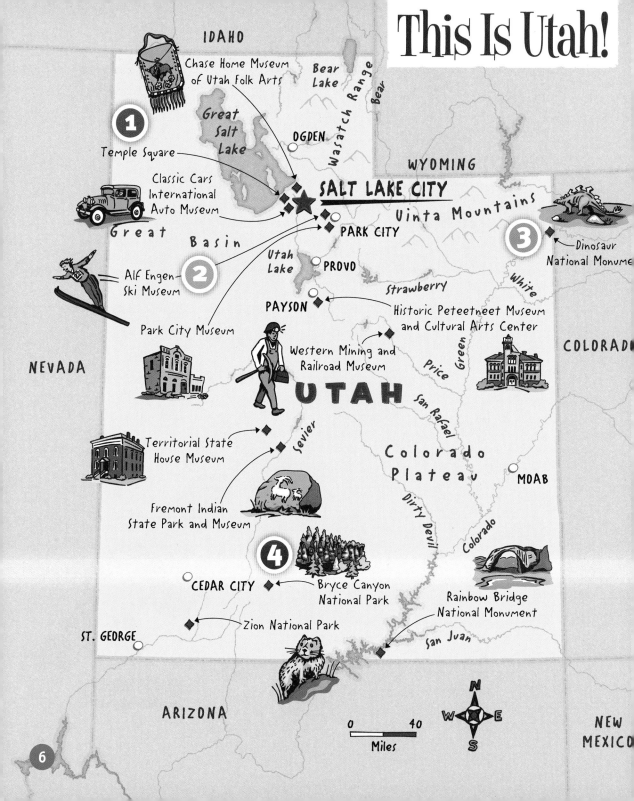

This Is Utah!

IDAHO

Chase Home Museum of Utah Folk Arts

Bear Lake

Wasatch Range

Bear

1

Great Salt Lake

Temple Square

OGDEN

WYOMING

Classic Cars International Auto Museum

★ SALT LAKE CITY

Uinta Mountains

3

Dinosaur National Monume

PARK CITY

Great   Basin

2

Utah Lake

PROVO

Alf Engen Ski Museum

Strawberry

White

PAYSON

Historic Peteetneet Museum and Cultural Arts Center

Park City Museum

Green

Price

COLORAD

NEVADA

Western Mining and Railroad Museum

UTAH

San Rafael

COLORADO

Territorial State House Museum

Sevier

Colorado Plateau

MOAB

Fremont Indian State Park and Museum

Dirty Devil

Colorado

4

CEDAR CITY

Bryce Canyon National Park

Rainbow Bridge National Monument

Zion National Park

ST. GEORGE

San Juan

ARIZONA

0   40
Miles

N
W   E
S

NEW MEXICO

1 Temple Square

This 10-acre (4-hectare) complex in Salt Lake City is a sacred place for the **Mormon** religion. It draws more visitors each year than any other attraction in Utah. People come to tour buildings such as the Salt Lake Temple.

2 Alf Engen Ski Museum

Utah's many mountains make it a popular destination for skiers. This museum in the ski town of Park City offers a virtual ski jump, artifacts from the sport's history, and more.

3 Dinosaur National Monument

Many dinosaur fossils have been discovered in Utah. At this park in the northeastern part of the state, visitors can view an enormous display of dinosaur fossils in a rock wall.

4 Bryce Canyon National Park

This park in southern Utah is famous for its many striped, strangely shaped rock pillars called hoodoos. **Erosion** shaped these fascinating rock formations over millions of years.

The Wasatch Range of the Rocky Mountains passes through north-central Utah.

CHAPTER 1

Land and Wildlife

Utah is a land of stunning natural beauty. Its landscapes range from snowcapped mountain peaks to the shimmering blue waters of the Great Salt Lake. Its sandy deserts are marked with dramatic canyons and rock formations unlike anything else on Earth. In other areas, there are green forests packed with plants and wildlife. It's no wonder that tourists come from around the world to glimpse this remarkable state.

Superb Scenery

Utah is in the heart of the American West. It borders six other states: Wyoming to the northeast, Colorado to the east, Arizona to the south, Nevada to the west, and Idaho to the north.

The state can be divided into three main geographical regions. The Basin and Range area lies in the western part of the state. Within this region's tall mountains and wide valleys is the famous Great Salt Lake. This is Utah's largest body of water.

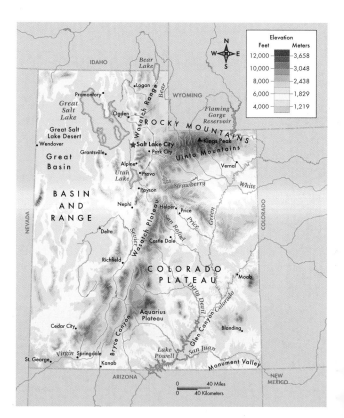

This map shows where the higher (orange) and lower (green) areas are in Utah.

The Great White Throne stands 2,394 feet (730 m) above the canyon floor below.

Zion National Park

Located in southwestern Utah, Zion National Park is home to some of the state's most dramatic scenery. Its most extreme feature is Zion Canyon. The canyon's green floor lies about 2,000 to 3,000 feet (610 to 914 meters) below the edges of the rocky cliffs. Also in the park is Kolob Arch, one of the world's largest stone arches. The Great White Throne, a mountain of white sandstone, towers over the park as well.

Kings Peak is located within the sprawling Ashley National Forest, which covers 1,287,909 acres (521,198 ha) of Utah land.

The Rocky Mountains run across northeastern Utah. Here, the state's tallest mountains tower high above the land. The tallest one of all is Kings Peak. Its **elevation** is 13,528 feet (4,123 m).

Southeastern Utah is part of the Colorado Plateau, the state's third geographical region. Utah's most incredible rock formations are located here. The Colorado and Green Rivers also run across the region. They are the longest waterways in the state.

Hot, Dry, and Sunny

Summers in Utah can be very hot, especially out in the desert. However, temperatures are usually nice and cool high up in the mountains, even during the warmest months.For the most part, Utah is a dry and sunny place. Only Nevada receives less **precipitation** than Utah. Because the state is so dry, Utah's ground cannot easily absorb water. This means that when it does rain, floods often occur.

MAXIMUM TEMPERATURE
117°F

MINIMUM TEMPERATURE
-50°F

Flash floods can cause soil to suddenly wash away, leading to the destruction of homes and other buildings.

Tall Trees and Colorful Flowers

A variety of trees grow in Utah's forests. Evergreens such as fir, spruce, pine, and juniper are especially common. These hardy trees often grow on mountainsides. Deserts have fewer trees, but there is still plenty that grows. Short plants such as grasses and sagebrush thrive in the dry climate. So do a variety of spiky cacti. Many of these plants produce colorful flowers that bloom each spring.

Cacti are especially common in the Colorado Plateau and the Basin and Range regions.

A Wild World

A huge number of animal species live in the wilderness. Black bears lumber through forests as hummingbirds zip through the air. Enormous moose and elk graze in grassy meadows. In deserts, snakes and other reptiles are common. Eagles, hawks, and other birds

A bull elk's antlers can stand up to 4 feet (1.2 m) above the elk's head.

of prey soar all across the state. Beavers share the state's waterways with aquatic birds such as geese and swans. The waters are also packed with fish, including trout, perch, and even goldfish.

Utah's capitol was built between 1912 and 1916.

CHAPTER 2

Government

When settlers arrived in what is now Utah in 1847, they made their home in the valley near the Great Salt Lake. Their settlement grew over time to become Salt Lake City. Ever since then, Salt Lake City has been Utah's most populous city and cultural center. Since 1856, it has also been the center of Utah's government. The capitol is located just north of downtown. Lawmakers from around the state gather in this building to work.

State Government

Utah's government, like other states and the **federal** government, has three branches. The executive branch is led by Utah's governor. It carries out state laws and oversees many important government duties, such as education and law enforcement. The legislative branch is made up of the Senate and the House of Representatives. It makes state laws. The judicial branch is the state court system. It hears cases and decides whether laws have been broken.

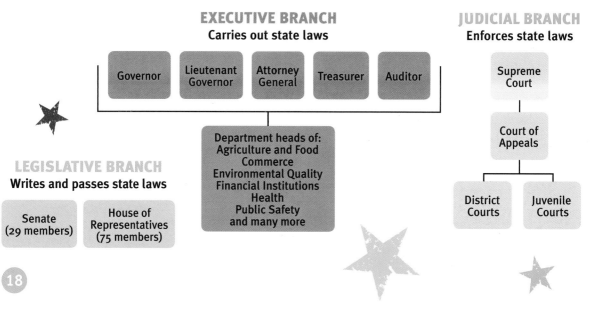

UTAH'S STATE GOVERNMENT

EXECUTIVE BRANCH
Carries out state laws

| Governor | Lieutenant Governor | Attorney General | Treasurer | Auditor |

Department heads of:
Agriculture and Food
Commerce
Environmental Quality
Financial Institutions
Health
Public Safety
and many more

JUDICIAL BRANCH
Enforces state laws

Supreme Court

Court of Appeals

District Courts — Juvenile Courts

LEGISLATIVE BRANCH
Writes and passes state laws

Senate (29 members) — House of Representatives (75 members)

Local Leadership

The state government oversees all of Utah as a whole. It does not, however, handle details that are specific to each individual section of the state. This is left to smaller local governments. Utah is divided into 29 counties,

A firefighter watches as a helicopter takes off to deliver water to a wildfire near Garden City.

each with its own government. Each county contains many towns and cities, which also have governments of their own. These local governments are important because they address issues specific to the people in that area of the state. They also oversee local services such as police and firefighters.

Utah in the National Government

Each state sends officials to represent it in the U.S. Congress. Like every state, Utah has two senators. The U.S. House of Representatives relies on a state's population to determine its numbers. Utah has four representatives in the House.

Every four years, states vote on the next U.S. president. Each state is granted a number of electoral votes based on its number of members in Congress. With two senators and four representatives, Utah has six electoral votes.

2 senators and 4 representatives

6 electoral votes

With six electoral votes, Utah's voice in presidential elections is below average compared to other states.

The People of Utah

Elected officials in Utah represent a population
with a range of interests, lifestyles, and backgrounds.

Ethnicity (2016 estimates)

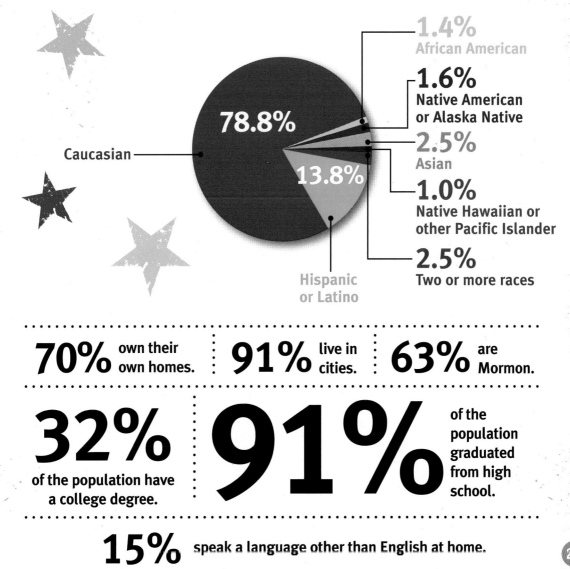

1.4%
African American

1.6%
Native American
or Alaska Native

2.5%
Asian

1.0%
Native Hawaiian or
other Pacific Islander

2.5%
Two or more races

78.8%

Caucasian

13.8%

Hispanic
or Latino

70% own their own homes.

91% live in cities.

63% are Mormon.

32% of the population have a college degree.

91% of the population graduated from high school.

15% speak a language other than English at home.

What Represents Utah?

States choose specific animals, plants, and objects to represent the values and characteristics of the land and its people. Find out why these symbols were chosen to represent Utah or discover surprising curiosities about them.

Seal

Utah's state seal has some common U.S. symbols, including a bald eagle and the U.S. flag. The two years shown are 1847, the year Mormon settlers arrived, and 1896, the year Utah became a state. The Beehive is the official state emblem and represents the hard work and industry of the state.

Flag

Utah's state flag displays the state seal on a blue field with a gold border.

Coal

STATE ROCK

There is a huge amount of coal under the surface of Utah. This valuable fuel can be found in 17 of Utah's 29 counties.

Dutch Oven

STATE COOKING POT

Early settlers in Utah used these heavy metal pots to cook food over fires. Many people still use them today.

Cherry

STATE FRUIT

Utah is one of the top states for cherry farming. Cherry trees cover about 4,800 acres (1,942 ha) of the state's land.

Rocky Mountain Elk

STATE ANIMAL

This huge mammal can be found nibbling on grass in the mountains of Utah.

Spanish Sweet Onion

STATE VEGETABLE

These tasty onions are grown on about 2,500 acres (1,012 ha) of Utah farmland.

California Seagull

STATE BIRD

Though this bird is named for the state of California, it is also a common sight near Utah's lakes.

Between 650 and 2,000 years ago, Ancestral Pueblo people made more than 650 carvings on Newspaper Rock.

CHAPTER 3

History

People have lived in what is now Utah for at least 12,000 years. The first people to arrive were a group called the Paleo-Indians. Around 6500 BCE, the Archaic people settled there, too. At the time, a huge lake covered much of the region. The Paleo-Indians and Archaic people lived along its shores. They fished in the lake and hunted using stone-tipped spears. They also gathered fruit and other wild plant foods.

Ancestral Pueblo dwellings at Mule Canyon in southeastern Utah were built more than 700 years ago.

Settling Down

Between 2,500 and 2,000 years ago, a new culture called the Ancestral Pueblo emerged in the Utah area. Unlike earlier Utah residents, they grew crops and raised turkeys on their farms. They also built large villages of buildings made from stone, **adobe**, and other materials. Some houses were dug into the ground. Others were freestanding or even carved into the sides of cliffs. No one is really sure why, but the Ancestral Pueblo left the area by about 1250 CE.

New Cultures

Not long after the mysterious exit of the Ancestral Pueblo, other groups began moving into present-day Utah. The Ute, Paiute, Goshute, and Shoshone peoples soon occupied much of the area. They were all part of a larger group called the Shoshonean people. They had similar languages and ways of life.

In about 1620, the Navajo people began moving into the region. Originally from Canada, they had already settled across much of the Southwest before coming to Utah.

This map shows some of the major tribes that lived in what is now Utah before Europeans came.

Settlers From Other Lands

In 1765, Spanish explorers became the first Europeans to arrive in what is now Utah. They considered the land part of the Spanish **colony** centered in present-day Mexico. However, the Spanish did not permanently settle in the area.

In the early 1800s, mountain men from the United States began coming to Utah to trap furs. As they explored, they created maps and blazed trails through the region.

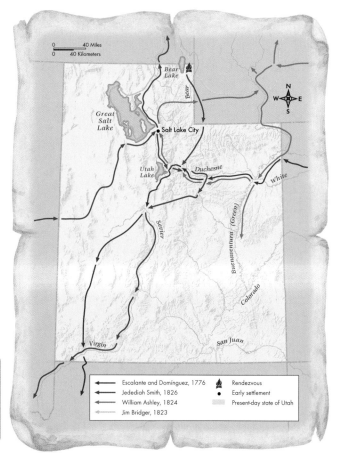

This map shows routes Europeans took as they explored and settled what is now Utah.

In 1847, a group of Mormon settlers led by Brigham Young arrived in the Salt Lake Valley. Mormons follow a religion started by Joseph Smith in New York State in 1830. For years, people had forced the Mormons out of each town they tried to settle in. Upon reaching Utah, they decided it was a good place to practice their religion in peace. Hoping to make a Mormon kingdom, they started building what would become Salt Lake City.

Mormon settlers in the 1800s built their homes from scratch using logs and other local materials.

Becoming a State

When the Mormons arrived, Utah belonged to Mexico. But the land soon fell under U.S. control after the Mexican-American War (1846–1848). Young had envisioned an independent Mormon kingdom. He realized, however, that the Mormons would have to compromise with the U.S. government. In 1850, the region officially became the U.S. territory of Utah. Young was its governor.

Timeline of Utah Events

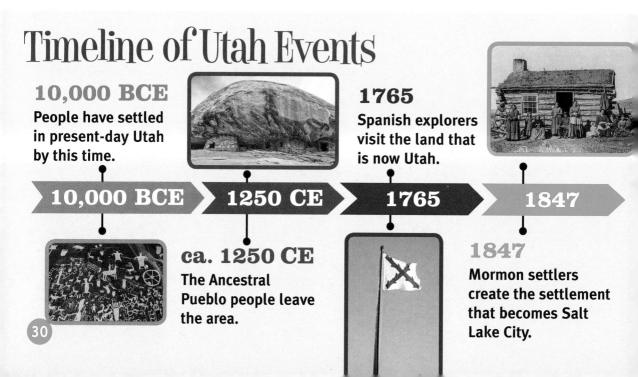

10,000 BCE
People have settled in present-day Utah by this time.

1765
Spanish explorers visit the land that is now Utah.

10,000 BCE	1250 CE	1765	1847

ca. 1250 CE
The Ancestral Pueblo people leave the area.

1847
Mormon settlers create the settlement that becomes Salt Lake City.

Disputes with the U.S. government over the Mormon practice of **polygamy** and other issues led to a conflict in 1858 called the Utah War. The two sides reached peace without violence. But U.S. leaders feared polygamy would spread. Over the following decades, Utah requested statehood and was rejected several times. Under this pressure, the Mormons outlawed polygamy in 1890, and Utah became the 45th state in 1896.

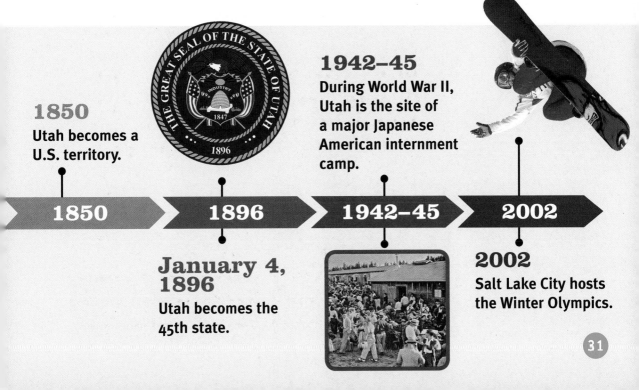

1850
Utah becomes a U.S. territory.

1942–45
During World War II, Utah is the site of a major Japanese American internment camp.

1850 **1896** **1942–45** **2002**

January 4, 1896
Utah becomes the 45th state.

2002
Salt Lake City hosts the Winter Olympics.

A Growing State

In the late 1800s and early 1900s, many **immigrants** came to Utah to work in coal, lead, and copper mines. They also helped build railroads. During World War I (1914–1918) and World War II (1939–1945), the mines became important sources for the materials needed to manufacture military supplies. In the following decades, the state continued to grow. More recently, it hosted the Winter Olympic Games in 2002.

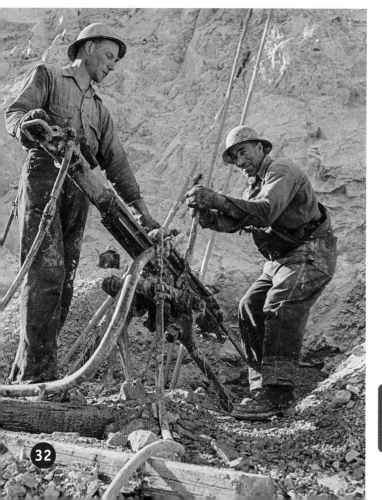

Workers use a rock drill to dig holes in a Utah copper mine in 1942.

Brigham Young

Born in Vermont in 1801, Brigham Young was an early follower of Joseph Smith and the Mormon faith. He quickly rose in the religion's leadership. When Smith was murdered in 1844, Young took command of the church. He began by leading a group of about 16,000 Mormons west in search of a permanent home. Under his guidance, the Mormons built many settlements in Utah. They also brought the first telegraph lines and railroads to the area.

Fourteen major ski resorts
are located in Utah.

CHAPTER 4

Culture

While large parts of Utah have few towns or people, other areas are jam-packed with activity. And even the state's most remote areas can be fun places for outdoor adventures. Utahns are diverse. Some are Native American or Latino families who have lived in the area for generations. Others are more recent arrivals from all around the world. Everyone brings something to the state, from a unique style of artwork to an old family cooking method.

Sports and Recreation

Utah sports fans have plenty to cheer. The Utah Jazz play basketball in Salt Lake City. The capital city also hosts two professional soccer teams, Real Salt Lake and Utah Royals FC. Many Utahns root for local college teams such as the Brigham Young University Cougars and the University of Utah Utes.

Outdoor activities are very popular. Snowy slopes draw skiers and snowboarders from around the world. People also love hiking and camping in Utah's outdoor areas.

The Jazz called New Orleans home for five seasons before settling in Utah in 1979.

Fairs and Festivals

Several exciting events keep the people of Utah entertained all year long. Each January, the movie industry's

About 200 films are screened each year at the Sundance Film Festival.

eyes are on Park City, where the famous Sundance Film Festival takes place. The event features films by independent filmmakers from around the world. It can turn unknown talents into Hollywood superstars. In September, crowds gather in Salt Lake City for the Utah State Fair. They try local foods, enjoy musical performances, and more.

Utah at Work

The people of Utah work in a wide range of industries. Many people provide important services to their fellow Utahns. These workers include teachers, doctors, waiters, and bankers. Others work in agriculture or mining. They raise livestock, grow crops, and gather materials such as coal and copper. Many Utahns are involved in manufacturing. They make everything from electronics and car parts to important medications.

A Growing Economy in a Growing State

Utah has a very strong **economy**. The average household income in the state is thousands of dollars above the national average. Utah also has one of the lowest **poverty** rates in the nation. And in 2016, more than twice as many new jobs were added here than in the average state. The construction and tourism industries were especially strong. As a result, Utah is attracting many new residents from other states and foreign countries alike.

Workers raise a wall on a house in Salt Lake City, where people are moving faster than enough new homes can be built.

Utah Cuisine

Utah cooks are influenced by the cultures that have existed in the area for generations. People love freshly grown squash, corn, and beans. All these foods have been staples since the early days of Native American settlement. Utahns also enjoy tacos, tamales, and other dishes brought by the state's Mexican population.

⭐ Utah Fry Sauce

Ask an adult to help you!

Out-of-town visitors might be surprised to see Utah locals dipping french fries in this tangy, pink-orange sauce instead of ketchup.

Ingredients

1 cup mayonnaise
1/2 cup ketchup
1 dill pickle, finely chopped

Directions

Mix all three ingredients together in a bowl until they are completely blended. Refrigerate the dip for at least an hour. Serve it alongside hot, crispy french fries or any other foods that normally go with ketchup. You can also try it on burgers and other sandwiches.

Hikers enjoy views of the amazing rock formations along Queens Garden Trail in Bryce Canyon National Park.

The Western Way of Life

From the rocky pillars and arches on the Colorado Plateau to the busy streets of downtown Salt Lake City, Utah is an amazing place to be. Whether people are visiting for the first time or their families have lived there for centuries, everyone appreciates the state's natural beauty, friendly residents, and rugged western lifestyle. Utah is truly a jewel of the West! ★

Famous People

Hal Ashby

(1929–1988) was a director whose classic films include *Harold and Maude* and *Being There*. He was from Ogden.

Robert Redford

(1936–) is a filmmaker and actor who has worked on countless Hollywood films. He founded the Sundance Film Festival, which is held each year in Park City.

Don Bluth

(1937–) is an animator and filmmaker who directed such films as *The Land Before Time*, *All Dogs Go to Heaven*, and *An American Tail*. He grew up in Payson.

Nolan Bushnell

(1943–) is an inventor and businessman who founded the Atari video game company and helped create the game Pong. He is also the creator of Chuck E. Cheese's restaurants. He is from Ogden.

Gedde Watanabe

(1955–) is an actor who has appeared in such films as *Sixteen Candles* and *Forgetting Sarah Marshall*, and lent his voice to the character of Ling in *Mulan*. He grew up in Ogden.

Steve Young

(1961–) is a retired National Football League quarterback who was twice chosen as the league's Most Valuable Player. He is now a member of the Pro Football Hall of Fame. He is a Salt Lake City native.

Karl Malone

(1963–) is a retired pro basketball player who is one of the highest-scoring players in National Basketball Association history. He played 18 seasons with the Utah Jazz.

Ken Jennings

(1974–) became famous when he went on a record-setting 74-game winning streak on the TV game show *Jeopardy!* He attended college at Brigham Young University and is a former resident of Salt Lake City.

Jewel Kilcher

(1974–) is an award-winning singer-songwriter and musician who has sold millions of records. She was born in Payson.

Chrissy Teigen

(1985–) is a model and the host of the show *Lip Sync Battle*. She is also the author of a best-selling cookbook. She was born in Delta.

Mary Elizabeth Winstead

(1984–) is an actor who has appeared in many movies, including *Scott Pilgrim vs. the World* and *10 Cloverfield Lane*. She lived in Sandy during her childhood.

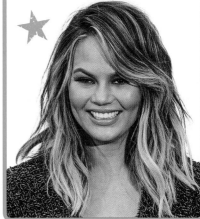

Did You Know That ...

There are five national parks in Utah: Arches National Park, Bryce Canyon National Park, Canyonlands National Park, Capitol Reef National Park, and Zion National Park. Only California and Alaska have more.

Utah is named for the Ute people, who have lived in the area since the 1300s.

The water in the Great Salt Lake is even saltier than ocean water. This high level of salt makes it extremely easy for a person to stay afloat while swimming.

Utah is one of the most sparsely populated states in the country. One big reason for this is the U.S. government owns about two-thirds of all the land in the state, including the national parks.

Many Hollywood filmmakers used to shoot their films in Utah. Its open areas and dramatic desert scenery make

it a perfect setting for movies that take place in the Old West.

The corners of Arizona, New Mexico, and Colorado all meet at the southeastern corner of Utah. This point, known as Four Corners, is the only location where four different U.S. states touch one another.

Utah's nickname is the Beehive State. This nickname came from the early Mormon settlers who built Salt Lake City. They thought their hard work was similar to the busy activity of bees in a beehive.

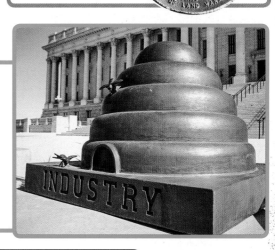

Did you find the truth?

F Brigham Young was the first European explorer to reach Utah.

T Utah was once a part of Mexico.

Resources

Books

Felix, Rebecca. *What's Great About Utah?* Minneapolis: Lerner Publications, 2015.

Kent, Deborah. *Utah.* New York: Children's Press, 2015.

Orr, Tamra B. *Zion.* New York: Children's Press, 2018.

Rozett, Louise (ed.). *Fast Facts About the 50 States: Plus Puerto Rico and Washington, D.C.* New York: Children's Press, 2010.

Visit this Scholastic website for more information on Utah:

★ www.factsfornow.scholastic.com
Enter the keyword **Utah**

Important Words

adobe (uh-DOH-bee) bricks made of clay mixed with straw and dried in the sun

colony (KAH-luh-nee) a territory that has been settled by people from another country and is controlled by that country

economy (ih-KAH-nuh-mee) the system of buying, selling, making things, and managing money in a place

elevation (el-uh-VAY-shuhn) the height above sea level

erosion (ih-ROH-zhuhn) the wearing away of something by water or wind

federal (FED-ur-uhl) having to do with the national U.S. government rather than a state or local government

immigrants (IM-ih-gruhnts) people who move from one country to another and settle there

Mormon (MOHR-muhn) a member of the Church of Jesus Christ of Latter-day Saints, a religion founded in New York in 1830 by Joseph Smith

polygamy (puh-LIG-uh-mee) a practice in which one person can marry multiple others

poverty (PAH-vur-tee) the state of being poor

precipitation (prih-sip-ih-TAY-shuhn) the falling of water from the sky in the form of rain, sleet, hail, or snow

Index

Page numbers in **bold** indicate illustrations.

About the Author

Josh Gregory is the author of more than 120 books for young readers. On visits to Utah, he has been amazed by the state's beautiful natural scenery. A former resident of Portland, Oregon, he currently lives in Chicago, Illinois.